ANXIETY JOURNAL

NAME ________________________

ADDRESS ________________________

PHONE ________________________

E-MAIL ________________________

MENTAL HEALTH MATTERS
SYMPTOMS OF ANXIETY

Anxiety affects not only our emotional state but also our daily life. You should never feel like you have to suffer in silence.

- **FEELING NERVOUS,**
- **RESTLESS OR TENSE.**
- **HAVING A SENSE OF IMPENDING DANGER,**
- **PANIC OR DOOM.**
- **HAVING AN INCREASED HEART RATE.**
- **BREATHING RAPIDLY (HYPERVENTILATION)**
- **SWEATING.**
- **TREMBLING.**
- **FEELING WEAK OR TIRED.**

LIST OF MY SYMPTOMS

____

____

____

____

____

How to Deal with Anxiety and Stress

1

Make Time for Yourself

2

Take Care of Your (Physical) Health

3

Give Yourself Time to Heal

Take time to do what makes your soul happy.

# Anxiety Journal

DATE & TIME _______________________________________

PLACE ______________________ SOURCE OF ANXIETY _______________________

NEGATIVE BELIEFS

ABOUT SITUATION:

ABOUT YOURSELF:

WHAT FACTS ARE TRUE

ABOUT SITUATION:

ABOUT YOURSELF:

WHAT HAPPENED AND HOW I FEEL

HOW DID I REACT & WHAT HELPS ME TO CALM

 Negative → Positive

My negative thought: _______________________

____

____

____

____

Evidence for my thought:

____

____

____

____

____

Evidence against my thought:

____

____

____

____

____

How can I reframe my negative thought to a more realistic one?

____

____

____

____

____

# Anxiety Journal

DATE & TIME ____

PLACE _____________________________ SOURCE OF ANXIETY _____________________________

NEGATIVE BELIEFS

ABOUT SITUATION:

ABOUT YOURSELF:

WHAT FACTS ARE TRUE

ABOUT SITUATION:

ABOUT YOURSELF:

WHAT HAPPENED AND HOW I FEEL

HOW DID I REACT & WHAT HELPS ME TO CALM

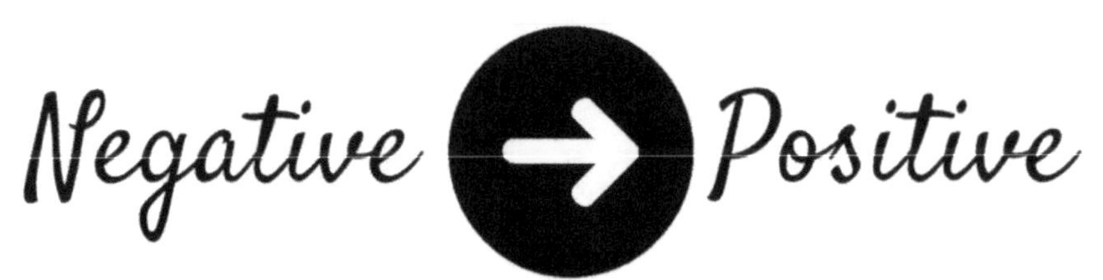

My negative thought: _______________________

____

____

____

____

Evidence for my thought:

Evidence against my thought:

How can I reframe my negative thought to a more realistic one?

Anxiety Journal

DATE & TIME ___________________________________

PLACE ____________________________ SOURCE OF ANXIETY ____________________

NEGATIVE BELIEFS

ABOUT SITUATION:

ABOUT YOURSELF:

WHAT FACTS ARE TRUE

ABOUT SITUATION:

ABOUT YOURSELF:

WHAT HAPPENED AND HOW I FEEL

HOW DID I REACT & WHAT HELPS ME TO CALM

My negative thought: _______________________________

____

____

____

____

Evidence for my thought:

Evidence against my thought:

How can I reframe my negative thought to a more realistic one?

____

____

____

____

Anxiety Journal

DATE & TIME ____

PLACE _____________________________ SOURCE OF ANXIETY _____________________________

NEGATIVE BELIEFS

ABOUT SITUATION:

ABOUT YOURSELF:

WHAT FACTS ARE TRUE

ABOUT SITUATION:

ABOUT YOURSELF:

WHAT HAPPENED AND HOW I FEEL

HOW DID I REACT & WHAT HELPS ME TO CALM

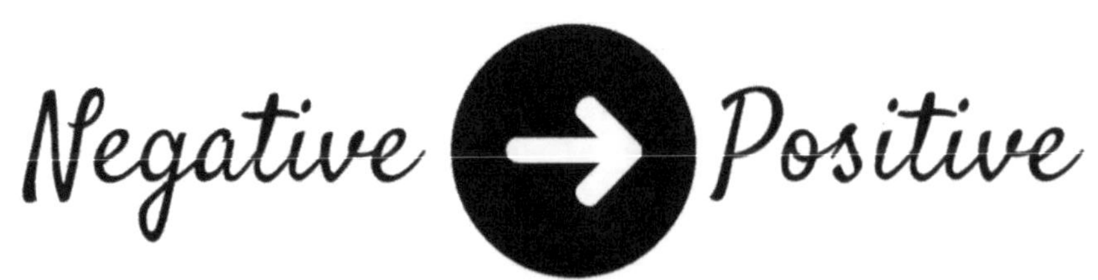

My negative thought: _______________________

____

____

____

____

Evidence for my thought:

Evidence against my thought:

How can I reframe my negative thought to a more realistic one?

Anxiety Journal

DATE & TIME _______________________________

PLACE _______________________ SOURCE OF ANXIETY _______________________

NEGATIVE BELIEFS

ABOUT SITUATION:

ABOUT YOURSELF:

WHAT FACTS ARE TRUE

ABOUT SITUATION:

ABOUT YOURSELF:

WHAT HAPPENED AND HOW I FEEL

HOW DID I REACT & WHAT HELPS ME TO CALM

 Negative → Positive

My negative thought: _______________________________
____
____
____
____

Evidence for my thought:

Evidence against my thought:

How can I reframe my negative thought to a more realistic one?

Anxiety Journal

DATE & TIME _______________________________________

PLACE _____________________ SOURCE OF ANXIETY _____________________

NEGATIVE BELIEFS

ABOUT SITUATION:

ABOUT YOURSELF:

WHAT FACTS ARE TRUE

ABOUT SITUATION:

ABOUT YOURSELF:

WHAT HAPPENED AND HOW I FEEL

HOW DID I REACT & WHAT HELPS ME TO CALM

Negative 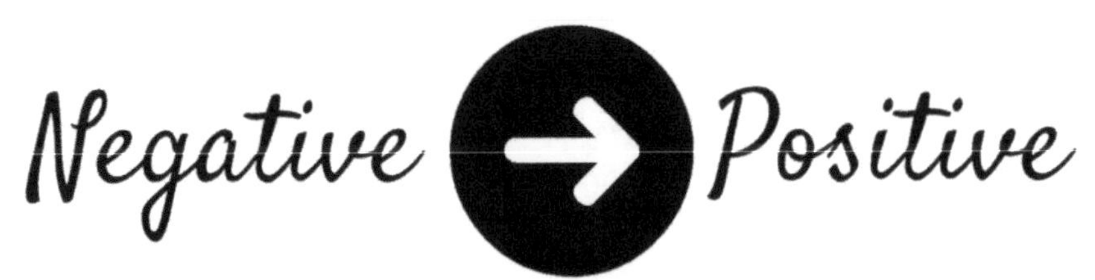 Positive

My negative thought: ___________________________

____
____
____
____

Evidence for my thought:

Evidence against my thought:

How can I reframe my negative thought to a more realistic one?

Anxiety Journal

DATE & TIME _______________________________________

PLACE _____________________________ SOURCE OF ANXIETY _____________________________

NEGATIVE BELIEFS

ABOUT SITUATION:

ABOUT YOURSELF:

WHAT FACTS ARE TRUE

ABOUT SITUATION:

ABOUT YOURSELF:

WHAT HAPPENED AND HOW I FEEL

HOW DID I REACT & WHAT HELPS ME TO CALM

My negative thought: _______________________
____
____
____
____

Evidence for my thought:

Evidence against my thought:

How can I reframe my negative thought to a more realistic one?

Anxiety Journal

DATE & TIME ___________________________

PLACE ___________________ SOURCE OF ANXIETY ___________________

ABOUT SITUATION:

ABOUT YOURSELF:

ABOUT SITUATION:

ABOUT YOURSELF:

My negative thought: _______________________

____

____

____

____

Evidence for my thought: Evidence against my thought:

How can I reframe my negative thought to a more realistic one?

____

____

____

____

Anxiety Journal

DATE & TIME ______________________________

PLACE ______________________ SOURCE OF ANXIETY ______________________

NEGATIVE BELIEFS

ABOUT SITUATION:

ABOUT YOURSELF:

WHAT FACTS ARE TRUE

ABOUT SITUATION:

ABOUT YOURSELF:

WHAT HAPPENED AND HOW I FEEL

HOW DID I REACT & WHAT HELPS ME TO CALM

My negative thought: _______________________

____

____

____

____

Evidence for my thought:

Evidence against my thought:

How can I reframe my negative thought to a more realistic one?

____

____

____

____

____

Anxiety Journal

DATE & TIME _______________________________

PLACE _____________________ SOURCE OF ANXIETY _____________________

NEGATIVE BELIEFS

ABOUT SITUATION:

ABOUT YOURSELF:

WHAT FACTS ARE TRUE

ABOUT SITUATION:

ABOUT YOURSELF:

WHAT HAPPENED AND HOW I FEEL

HOW DID I REACT & WHAT HELPS ME TO CALM

Negative → Positive

My negative thought: _______________________

____

____

____

____

Evidence for my thought:

Evidence against my thought:

How can I reframe my negative thought to a more realistic one?

____

____

____

____

____

Anxiety Journal

DATE & TIME ____

PLACE ______________________ SOURCE OF ANXIETY ________________________

NEGATIVE BELIEFS

ABOUT SITUATION:

ABOUT YOURSELF:

WHAT FACTS ARE TRUE

ABOUT SITUATION:

ABOUT YOURSELF:

WHAT HAPPENED AND HOW I FEEL

HOW DID I REACT & WHAT HELPS ME TO CALM

 Negative → Positive

My negative thought: _______________________

____

____

____

____

Evidence for my thought:

Evidence against my thought:

How can I reframe my negative thought to a more realistic one?

Anxiety Journal

DATE & TIME ______________________________

PLACE ______________________ SOURCE OF ANXIETY ______________________

NEGATIVE BELIEFS

ABOUT SITUATION:

ABOUT YOURSELF:

WHAT FACTS ARE TRUE

ABOUT SITUATION:

ABOUT YOURSELF:

WHAT HAPPENED AND HOW I FEEL

HOW DID I REACT & WHAT HELPS ME TO CALM

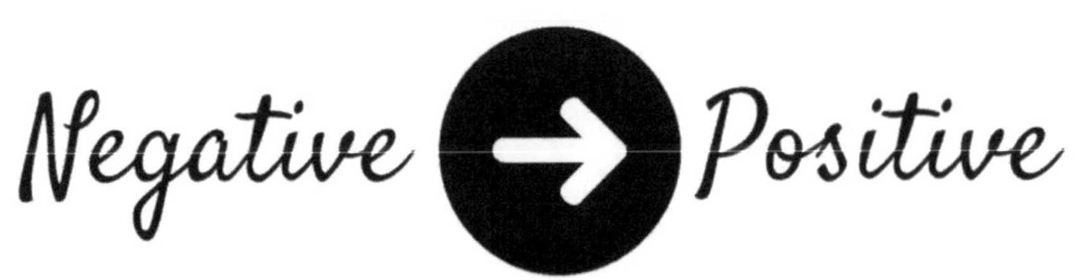 Negative → Positive

My negative thought: _______________________

____

____

____

____

Evidence for my thought:

Evidence against my thought:

How can I reframe my negative thought to a more realistic one?

 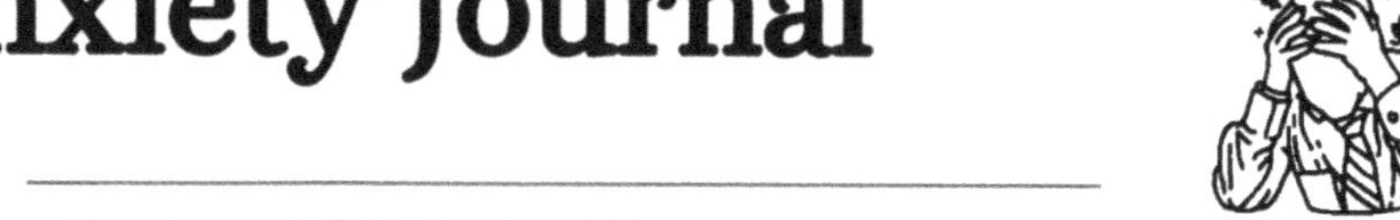 

Anxiety Journal

DATE & TIME _______________________________________

PLACE _______________________ SOURCE OF ANXIETY _______________________

NEGATIVE BELIEFS

ABOUT SITUATION:

ABOUT YOURSELF:

WHAT FACTS ARE TRUE

ABOUT SITUATION:

ABOUT YOURSELF:

WHAT HAPPENED AND HOW I FEEL

HOW DID I REACT & WHAT HELPS ME TO CALM

My negative thought: _______________________

____

____

____

____

Evidence for my thought:

Evidence against my thought:

How can I reframe my negative thought to a more realistic one?

____

____

____

____

____

# Anxiety Journal

DATE & TIME _________________________________

PLACE _____________________ SOURCE OF ANXIETY _____________________

NEGATIVE BELIEFS

ABOUT SITUATION:

ABOUT YOURSELF:

WHAT FACTS ARE TRUE

ABOUT SITUATION:

ABOUT YOURSELF:

WHAT HAPPENED AND HOW I FEEL

HOW DID I REACT & WHAT HELPS ME TO CALM

Negative → Positive

My negative thought: ___________________________

____

____

____

____

Evidence for my thought:

Evidence against my thought:

How can I reframe my negative thought to a more realistic one?

Anxiety Journal

DATE & TIME  _______________________________

PLACE _______________________ SOURCE OF ANXIETY _______________________

NEGATIVE BELIEFS

ABOUT SITUATION:

ABOUT YOURSELF:

WHAT FACTS ARE TRUE

ABOUT SITUATION:

ABOUT YOURSELF:

WHAT HAPPENED AND HOW I FEEL

HOW DID I REACT & WHAT HELPS ME TO CALM

 Negative → Positive

My negative thought: _______________________________

____

____

____

____

Evidence for my thought:

Evidence against my thought:

How can I reframe my negative thought to a more realistic one?

Anxiety Journal

DATE & TIME __________________________________

PLACE _____________________ SOURCE OF ANXIETY __________________________

NEGATIVE BELIEFS

ABOUT SITUATION:

ABOUT YOURSELF:

WHAT FACTS ARE TRUE

ABOUT SITUATION:

ABOUT YOURSELF:

WHAT HAPPENED AND HOW I FEEL

HOW DID I REACT & WHAT HELPS ME TO CALM

Negative → Positive

My negative thought: _______________________________

____

____

____

Evidence for my thought:

Evidence against my thought:

How can I reframe my negative thought to a more realistic one?

Anxiety Journal

DATE & TIME _______________________________

PLACE ____________________________ SOURCE OF ANXIETY _______________________

NEGATIVE BELIEFS

ABOUT SITUATION:

ABOUT YOURSELF:

WHAT FACTS ARE TRUE

ABOUT SITUATION:

ABOUT YOURSELF:

WHAT HAPPENED AND HOW I FEEL

HOW DID I REACT & WHAT HELPS ME TO CALM

 Negative → Positive

My negative thought: _______________________________
____
____
____
____

Evidence for my thought:

Evidence against my thought:

____
____
____
____

Anxiety Journal

DATE & TIME _______________________________

PLACE _______________________ SOURCE OF ANXIETY _______________________

NEGATIVE BELIEFS

ABOUT SITUATION:

ABOUT YOURSELF:

WHAT FACTS ARE TRUE

ABOUT SITUATION:

ABOUT YOURSELF:

WHAT HAPPENED AND HOW I FEEL

HOW DID I REACT & WHAT HELPS ME TO CALM

Negative → Positive

My negative thought: _______________________

____

____

____

Evidence for my thought:

Evidence against my thought:

How can I reframe my negative thought to a more realistic one?

____

____

____

____

____

Anxiety Journal

DATE & TIME ___________________________________

PLACE _______________________________ SOURCE OF ANXIETY _______________________________

NEGATIVE BELIEFS

ABOUT SITUATION:

ABOUT YOURSELF:

WHAT FACTS ARE TRUE

ABOUT SITUATION:

ABOUT YOURSELF:

WHAT HAPPENED AND HOW I FEEL

HOW DID I REACT & WHAT HELPS ME TO CALM

 Negative → Positive

My negative thought: ___________________________

____

____

____

____

Evidence for my thought:

Evidence against my thought:

How can I reframe my negative thought to a more realistic one?

Anxiety Journal

DATE & TIME _______________________________________

PLACE ___________________________ SOURCE OF ANXIETY ___________________________

NEGATIVE BELIEFS

ABOUT SITUATION:

ABOUT YOURSELF:

WHAT FACTS ARE TRUE

ABOUT SITUATION:

ABOUT YOURSELF:

WHAT HAPPENED AND HOW I FEEL

HOW DID I REACT & WHAT HELPS ME TO CALM

Negative → Positive

My negative thought: _______________________
____
____
____
____

Evidence for my thought:

Evidence against my thought:

How can I reframe my negative thought to a more realistic one?

Anxiety Journal

DATE & TIME _______________________________________

PLACE _______________________ SOURCE OF ANXIETY _______________________

NEGATIVE BELIEFS

ABOUT SITUATION:

ABOUT YOURSELF:

WHAT FACTS ARE TRUE

ABOUT SITUATION:

ABOUT YOURSELF:

WHAT HAPPENED AND HOW I FEEL

HOW DID I REACT & WHAT HELPS ME TO CALM

 Negative → Positive

My negative thought: _______________________

____
____
____
____

Evidence for my thought:

Evidence against my thought:

How can I reframe my negative thought to a more realistic one?

____
____
____
____

Anxiety Journal

DATE & TIME ____

PLACE ______________________________ SOURCE OF ANXIETY ______________________

NEGATIVE BELIEFS

ABOUT SITUATION:

ABOUT YOURSELF:

WHAT FACTS ARE TRUE

ABOUT SITUATION:

ABOUT YOURSELF:

WHAT HAPPENED AND HOW I FEEL

HOW DID I REACT & WHAT HELPS ME TO CALM

Negative  Positive

My negative thought: ______________________________

____

____

____

Evidence for my thought: Evidence against my thought:

How can I reframe my negative thought to a more realistic one?

Anxiety Journal

DATE & TIME ______________________________

PLACE ______________________ SOURCE OF ANXIETY ______________________

NEGATIVE BELIEFS

ABOUT SITUATION:

ABOUT YOURSELF:

WHAT FACTS ARE TRUE

ABOUT SITUATION:

ABOUT YOURSELF:

WHAT HAPPENED AND HOW I FEEL

HOW DID I REACT & WHAT HELPS ME TO CALM

Negative 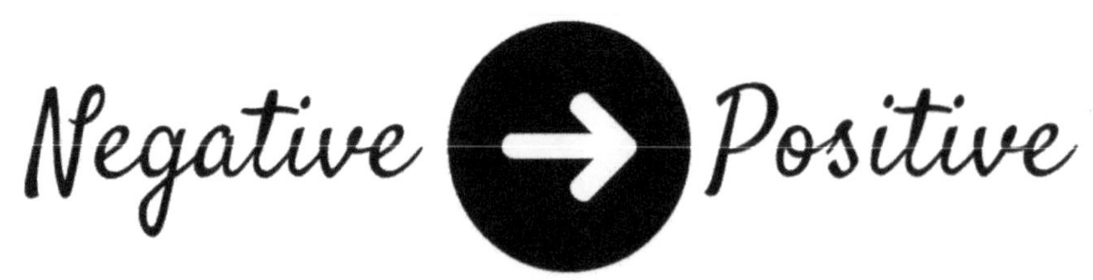 Positive

My negative thought: _______________________

____

____

____

____

Evidence for my thought:

Evidence against my thought:

How can I reframe my negative thought to a more realistic one?

Anxiety Journal

DATE & TIME __________________________________

PLACE ____________________ SOURCE OF ANXIETY ____________________

NEGATIVE BELIEFS

ABOUT SITUATION:

ABOUT YOURSELF:

WHAT FACTS ARE TRUE

ABOUT SITUATION:

ABOUT YOURSELF:

WHAT HAPPENED AND HOW I FEEL

HOW DID I REACT & WHAT HELPS ME TO CALM

Negative  Positive

My negative thought: _______________________

____

____

____

____

Evidence for my thought: Evidence against my thought:

How can I reframe my negative thought to a more realistic one?

Anxiety Journal

DATE & TIME _______________________________

PLACE _____________________________ SOURCE OF ANXIETY _______________________

NEGATIVE BELIEFS

ABOUT SITUATION:

ABOUT YOURSELF:

WHAT FACTS ARE TRUE

ABOUT SITUATION:

ABOUT YOURSELF:

WHAT HAPPENED AND HOW I FEEL

HOW DID I REACT & WHAT HELPS ME TO CALM

My negative thought: _______________________________

____

____

____

____

Evidence for my thought:

Evidence against my thought:

How can I reframe my negative thought to a more realistic one?

____

____

____

____

____

Anxiety Journal

DATE & TIME ___________________________

PLACE _____________________ SOURCE OF ANXIETY ___________________________

NEGATIVE BELIEFS

ABOUT SITUATION:

ABOUT YOURSELF:

WHAT FACTS ARE TRUE

ABOUT SITUATION:

ABOUT YOURSELF:

WHAT HAPPENED AND HOW I FEEL

HOW DID I REACT & WHAT HELPS ME TO CALM

Negative  Positive

My negative thought: _______________________

____

____

____

____

Evidence for my thought:

Evidence against my thought:

How can I reframe my negative thought to a more realistic one?

 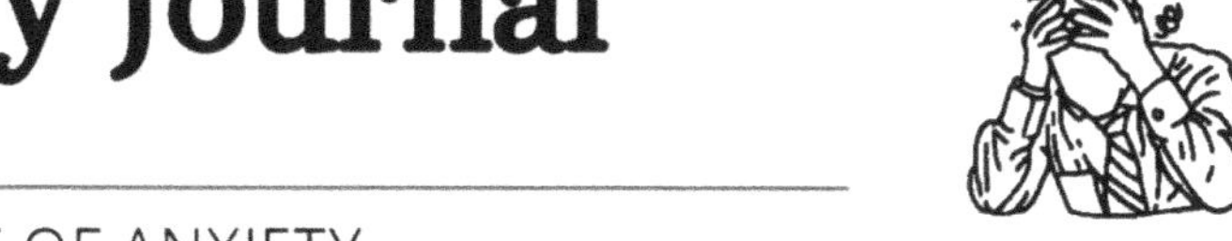

Anxiety Journal

DATE & TIME _______________________________

PLACE _______________________ SOURCE OF ANXIETY _______________________

NEGATIVE BELIEFS

ABOUT SITUATION:

ABOUT YOURSELF:

WHAT FACTS ARE TRUE

ABOUT SITUATION:

ABOUT YOURSELF:

WHAT HAPPENED AND HOW I FEEL

HOW DID I REACT & WHAT HELPS ME TO CALM

Negative  Positive

My negative thought: _______________________________

____

____

____

____

Evidence for my thought:

Evidence against my thought:

How can I reframe my negative thought to a more realistic one?

Anxiety Journal

DATE & TIME _______________________________________

PLACE ___________________________ SOURCE OF ANXIETY _______________________

NEGATIVE BELIEFS

ABOUT SITUATION:

ABOUT YOURSELF:

WHAT FACTS ARE TRUE

ABOUT SITUATION:

ABOUT YOURSELF:

WHAT HAPPENED AND HOW I FEEL

HOW DID I REACT & WHAT HELPS ME TO CALM

Negative 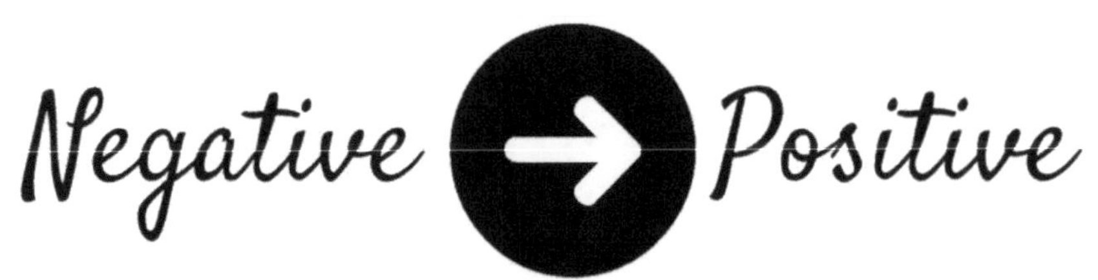 Positive

My negative thought: _______________________

____

____

____

____

Evidence for my thought:

Evidence against my thought:

How can I reframe my negative thought to a more realistic one?

Anxiety Journal

DATE & TIME _______________________________

PLACE _____________________ SOURCE OF ANXIETY _____________________

NEGATIVE BELIEFS

ABOUT SITUATION:

ABOUT YOURSELF:

WHAT FACTS ARE TRUE

ABOUT SITUATION:

ABOUT YOURSELF:

WHAT HAPPENED AND HOW I FEEL

HOW DID I REACT & WHAT HELPS ME TO CALM

Negative  Positive

My negative thought: _______________________________

____

____

____

____

Evidence for my thought:

Evidence against my thought:

How can I reframe my negative thought to a more realistic one?

Anxiety Journal

DATE & TIME _______________________________

PLACE _______________________   SOURCE OF ANXIETY _______________________

NEGATIVE BELIEFS

ABOUT SITUATION:

ABOUT YOURSELF:

WHAT FACTS ARE TRUE

ABOUT SITUATION:

ABOUT YOURSELF:

WHAT HAPPENED AND HOW I FEEL

HOW DID I REACT & WHAT HELPS ME TO CALM

Negative → Positive

My negative thought: ____

____

____

____

Evidence for my thought:

____

____

____

____

____

____

Evidence against my thought:

____

____

____

____

____

____

How can I reframe my negative thought to a more realistic one?

____

____

____

____

____

Anxiety Journal

DATE & TIME ____

PLACE ___________________________ SOURCE OF ANXIETY ___________________________

NEGATIVE BELIFS

ABOUT SITUATION:

ABOUT YOURSELF:

WHAT FACTS ARE TRUE

ABOUT SITUATION:

ABOUT YOURSELF:

WHAT HAPPENED AND HOW I FEEL

HOW DID I REACT & WHAT HELPS ME TO CALM

 Negative → Positive

My negative thought: ________________________

____

____

____

____

Evidence for my thought:

Evidence against my thought:

How can I reframe my negative thought to a more realistic one?

Anxiety Journal

DATE & TIME _______________________________

PLACE _____________________ SOURCE OF ANXIETY _____________________

NEGATIVE BELIEFS

ABOUT SITUATION:

ABOUT YOURSELF:

WHAT FACTS ARE TRUE

ABOUT SITUATION:

ABOUT YOURSELF:

WHAT HAPPENED AND HOW I FEEL

HOW DID I REACT & WHAT HELPS ME TO CALM

My negative thought: ______________________
____
____
____
____

Evidence for my thought:

Evidence against my thought:

How can I reframe my negative thought to a more realistic one?

Anxiety Journal

DATE & TIME _______________________________

PLACE _______________________ SOURCE OF ANXIETY _______________________

NEGATIVE BELIEFS

ABOUT SITUATION:

ABOUT YOURSELF:

WHAT FACTS ARE TRUE

ABOUT SITUATION:

ABOUT YOURSELF:

WHAT HAPPENED AND HOW I FEEL

HOW DID I REACT & WHAT HELPS ME TO CALM

Negative 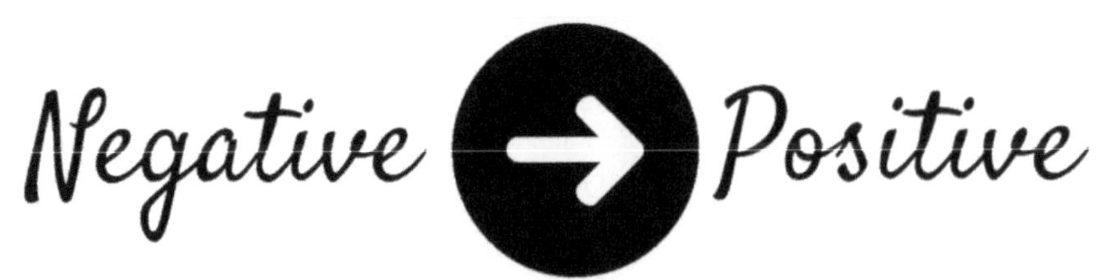 Positive

My negative thought: ______________________

____

____

____

____

Evidence for my thought:

Evidence against my thought:

How can I reframe my negative thought to a more realistic one?

Anxiety Journal

DATE & TIME _______________________________

PLACE _______________________ SOURCE OF ANXIETY _______________________

NEGATIVE BELIEFS

ABOUT SITUATION:

ABOUT YOURSELF:

WHAT FACTS ARE TRUE

ABOUT SITUATION:

ABOUT YOURSELF:

WHAT HAPPENED AND HOW I FEEL

HOW DID I REACT & WHAT HELPS ME TO CALM

Negative → Positive

My negative thought: _______________________

Evidence for my thought: Evidence against my thought:

How can I reframe my negative thought to a more realistic one?

# Anxiety Journal

DATE & TIME ___________________________________

PLACE ____________________________ SOURCE OF ANXIETY ____________________________

NEGATIVE BELIEFS

ABOUT SITUATION:

ABOUT YOURSELF:

WHAT FACTS ARE TRUE

ABOUT SITUATION:

ABOUT YOURSELF:

WHAT HAPPENED AND HOW I FEEL

HOW DID I REACT & WHAT HELPS ME TO CALM

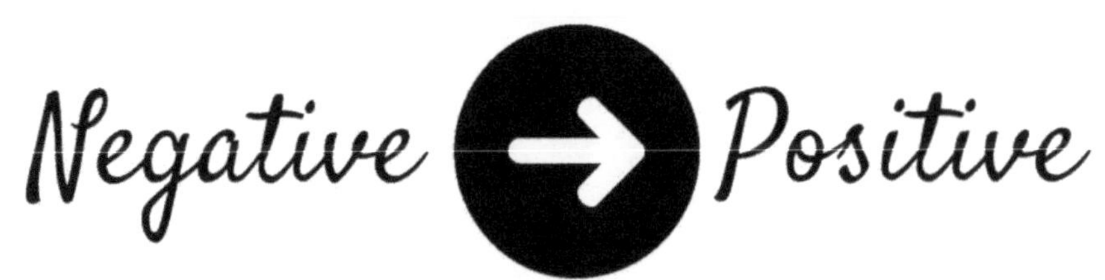

My negative thought: _______________________

____

____

____

____

Evidence for my thought:

Evidence against my thought:

How can I reframe my negative thought to a more realistic one?

Anxiety Journal

DATE & TIME _______________________________

PLACE _____________________ SOURCE OF ANXIETY _______________

NEGATIVE BELIEFS

ABOUT SITUATION:

ABOUT YOURSELF:

WHAT FACTS ARE TRUE

ABOUT SITUATION:

ABOUT YOURSELF:

WHAT HAPPENED AND HOW I FEEL

HOW DID I REACT & WHAT HELPS ME TO CALM

Negative 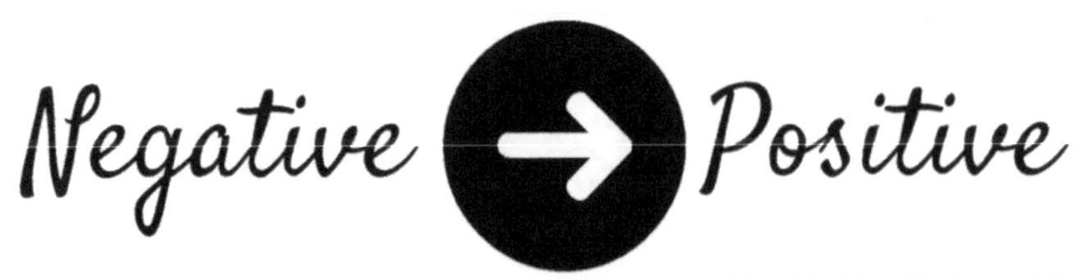 Positive

My negative thought: _______________________

____

____

____

____

Evidence for my thought:

Evidence against my thought:

How can I reframe my negative thought to a more realistic one?

Anxiety Journal

DATE & TIME _______________________________

PLACE ___________________________ SOURCE OF ANXIETY _______________________

NEGATIVE BELIEFS

ABOUT SITUATION:

ABOUT YOURSELF:

WHAT FACTS ARE TRUE

ABOUT SITUATION:

ABOUT YOURSELF:

WHAT HAPPENED AND HOW I FEEL

HOW DID I REACT & WHAT HELPS ME TO CALM

Negative  Positive

My negative thought: ______________________

____

Evidence for my thought:

Evidence against my thought:

How can I reframe my negative thought to a more realistic one?

Anxiety Journal

DATE & TIME ____

PLACE ____________________________ SOURCE OF ANXIETY ____________________________

NEGATIVE BELIEFS

ABOUT SITUATION:

ABOUT YOURSELF:

WHAT FACTS ARE TRUE

ABOUT SITUATION:

ABOUT YOURSELF:

WHAT HAPPENED AND HOW I FEEL

HOW DID I REACT & WHAT HELPS ME TO CALM

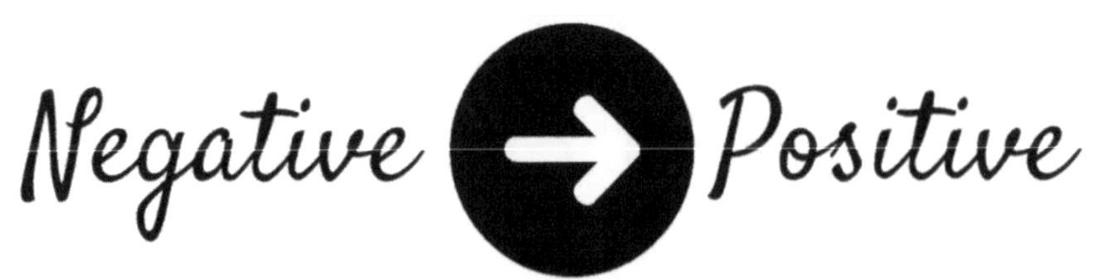 Negative → Positive

My negative thought: _______________________

____

____

____

____

Evidence for my thought:

Evidence against my thought:

How can I reframe my negative thought to a more realistic one?

Anxiety Journal

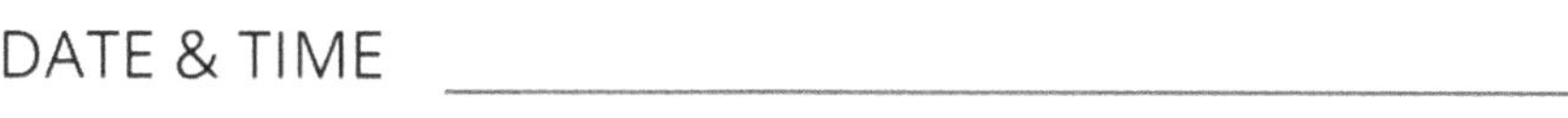

DATE & TIME _______________________________

PLACE _______________________ SOURCE OF ANXIETY _______________________

NEGATIVE BELIEFS

ABOUT SITUATION:

ABOUT YOURSELF:

WHAT FACTS ARE TRUE

ABOUT SITUATION:

ABOUT YOURSELF:

WHAT HAPPENED AND HOW I FEEL

HOW DID I REACT & WHAT HELPS ME TO CALM

Negative → Positive

My negative thought: _______________________

____

____

____

____

Evidence for my thought:

Evidence against my thought:

How can I reframe my negative thought to a more realistic one?

Anxiety Journal

DATE & TIME _______________________________

PLACE _______________________ SOURCE OF ANXIETY _______________________

NEGATIVE BELIEFS

ABOUT SITUATION:

ABOUT YOURSELF:

WHAT FACTS ARE TRUE

ABOUT SITUATION:

ABOUT YOURSELF:

WHAT HAPPENED AND HOW I FEEL

HOW DID I REACT & WHAT HELPS ME TO CALM

Negative  Positive

My negative thought: _______________________________

____

____

____

____

Evidence for my thought:

Evidence against my thought:

How can I reframe my negative thought to a more realistic one?

# Anxiety Journal

DATE & TIME ____

PLACE ____________________________ SOURCE OF ANXIETY ____________________________

NEGATIVE BELIEFS

ABOUT SITUATION:

ABOUT YOURSELF:

WHAT FACTS ARE TRUE

ABOUT SITUATION:

ABOUT YOURSELF:

WHAT HAPPENED AND HOW I FEEL

HOW DID I REACT & WHAT HELPS ME TO CALM

Negative  Positive

My negative thought: __________________________

____

____

____

____

Evidence for my thought:

Evidence against my thought:

How can I reframe my negative thought to a more realistic one?

____

____

____

____

____

Anxiety Journal

DATE & TIME _______________________________

PLACE _____________________ SOURCE OF ANXIETY _____________________

NEGATIVE BELIEFS

ABOUT SITUATION:

ABOUT YOURSELF:

WHAT FACTS ARE TRUE

ABOUT SITUATION:

ABOUT YOURSELF:

WHAT HAPPENED AND HOW I FEEL

HOW DID I REACT & WHAT HELPS ME TO CALM

 Negative → Positive

My negative thought: ____________________

____

____

____

____

Evidence for my thought:

Evidence against my thought:

How can I reframe my negative thought to a more realistic one?

Anxiety Journal

DATE & TIME ___________________________________

PLACE _______________________ SOURCE OF ANXIETY _______________________

NEGATIVE BELIEFS

ABOUT SITUATION:

ABOUT YOURSELF:

WHAT FACTS ARE TRUE

ABOUT SITUATION:

ABOUT YOURSELF:

WHAT HAPPENED AND HOW I FEEL

HOW DID I REACT & WHAT HELPS ME TO CALM

My negative thought: _______________________

____

____

____

____

Evidence for my thought:

Evidence against my thought:

How can I reframe my negative thought to a more realistic one?

Anxiety Journal

DATE & TIME ______________________________

PLACE ___________________ SOURCE OF ANXIETY ______________________

NEGATIVE BELIEFS

ABOUT SITUATION:

ABOUT YOURSELF:

WHAT FACTS ARE TRUE

ABOUT SITUATION:

ABOUT YOURSELF:

WHAT HAPPENED AND HOW I FEEL

HOW DID I REACT & WHAT HELPS ME TO CALM

Negative → Positive

My negative thought: _______________________________

____

____

____

____

Evidence for my thought:

Evidence against my thought:

How can I reframe my negative thought to a more realistic one?

Anxiety Journal

DATE & TIME ____

PLACE ___________________________ SOURCE OF ANXIETY ___________________________

NEGATIVE BELIEFS

ABOUT SITUATION:

ABOUT YOURSELF:

WHAT FACTS ARE TRUE

ABOUT SITUATION:

ABOUT YOURSELF:

WHAT HAPPENED AND HOW I FEEL

HOW DID I REACT & WHAT HELPS ME TO CALM

Negative  Positive

My negative thought: _______________________

____

____

____

____

Evidence for my thought:

Evidence against my thought:

How can I reframe my negative thought to a more realistic one?

____

____

____

____

Anxiety Journal

DATE & TIME _______________________________

PLACE _______________________ SOURCE OF ANXIETY _______________________

NEGATIVE BELIEFS

ABOUT SITUATION:

ABOUT YOURSELF:

WHAT FACTS ARE TRUE

ABOUT SITUATION:

ABOUT YOURSELF:

WHAT HAPPENED AND HOW I FEEL

HOW DID I REACT & WHAT HELPS ME TO CALM

Negative → Positive

My negative thought: _______________

____
____
____
____

Evidence for my thought:

Evidence against my thought:

How can I reframe my negative thought to a more realistic one?

____
____
____
____

Anxiety Journal

DATE & TIME ________________________________

PLACE ______________________ SOURCE OF ANXIETY ______________________

NEGATIVE BELIEFS

ABOUT SITUATION:

ABOUT YOURSELF:

WHAT FACTS ARE TRUE

ABOUT SITUATION:

ABOUT YOURSELF:

WHAT HAPPENED AND HOW I FEEL

HOW DID I REACT & WHAT HELPS ME TO CALM

Negative  Positive

My negative thought: _______________________

____

____

____

____

Evidence for my thought:

Evidence against my thought:

How can I reframe my negative thought to a more realistic one?

# Anxiety Journal

DATE & TIME ___________________________

PLACE ___________________________ SOURCE OF ANXIETY ___________________________

NEGATIVE BELIEFS

ABOUT SITUATION:

ABOUT YOURSELF:

WHAT FACTS ARE TRUE

ABOUT SITUATION:

ABOUT YOURSELF:

WHAT HAPPENED AND HOW I FEEL

HOW DID I REACT & WHAT HELPS ME TO CALM

Negative → Positive

My negative thought: _______________________

____

____

____

____

Evidence for my thought:

Evidence against my thought:

How can I reframe my negative thought to a more realistic one?

____

____

____

____

____

Anxiety Journal

DATE & TIME _______________________________________

PLACE _______________________ SOURCE OF ANXIETY _______________________

NEGATIVE BELIEFS

ABOUT SITUATION:

ABOUT YOURSELF:

WHAT FACTS ARE TRUE

ABOUT SITUATION:

ABOUT YOURSELF:

WHAT HAPPENED AND HOW I FEEL

HOW DID I REACT & WHAT HELPS ME TO CALM

Negative  Positive

My negative thought: _______________________

____

____

____

____

Evidence for my thought:

Evidence against my thought:

How can I reframe my negative thought to a more realistic one?

Anxiety Journal

DATE & TIME _______________________________

PLACE ___________________________ SOURCE OF ANXIETY ___________________________

NEGATIVE BELIEFS

ABOUT SITUATION:

ABOUT YOURSELF:

WHAT FACTS ARE TRUE

ABOUT SITUATION:

ABOUT YOURSELF:

WHAT HAPPENED AND HOW I FEEL

HOW DID I REACT & WHAT HELPS ME TO CALM

Negative 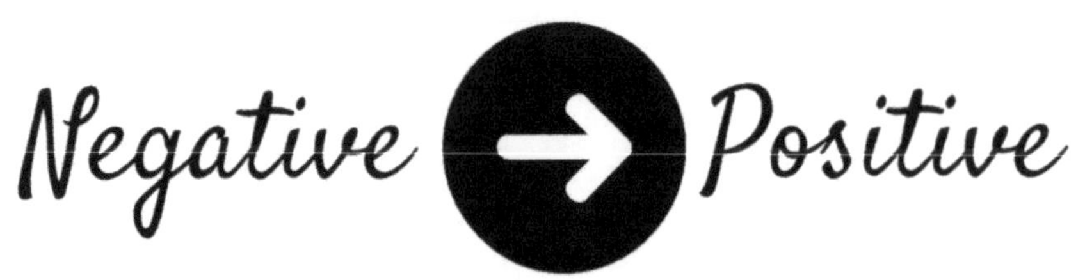 Positive

My negative thought: _______________________

____

____

____

Evidence for my thought:

Evidence against my thought:

How can I reframe my negative thought to a more realistic one?

____

____

____

____

Anxiety Journal

DATE & TIME _______________________________

PLACE _______________________ SOURCE OF ANXIETY _______________________

NEGATIVE BELIEFS

ABOUT SITUATION:

ABOUT YOURSELF:

WHAT FACTS ARE TRUE

ABOUT SITUATION:

ABOUT YOURSELF:

WHAT HAPPENED AND HOW I FEEL

HOW DID I REACT & WHAT HELPS ME TO CALM

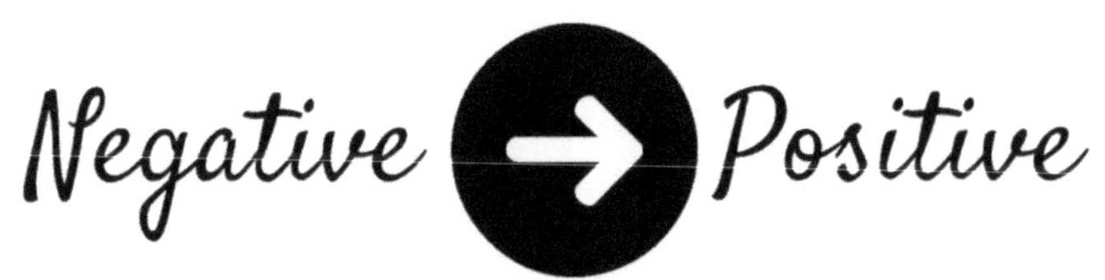 Negative → Positive

My negative thought: _______________________________

____

____

____

____

Evidence for my thought:

Evidence against my thought:

How can I reframe my negative thought to a more realistic one?

Anxiety Journal

DATE & TIME _______________________________________

PLACE _______________________ SOURCE OF ANXIETY _______________________

NEGATIVE BELIEFS

ABOUT SITUATION:

ABOUT YOURSELF:

WHAT FACTS ARE TRUE

ABOUT SITUATION:

ABOUT YOURSELF:

WHAT HAPPENED AND HOW I FEEL

HOW DID I REACT & WHAT HELPS ME TO CALM

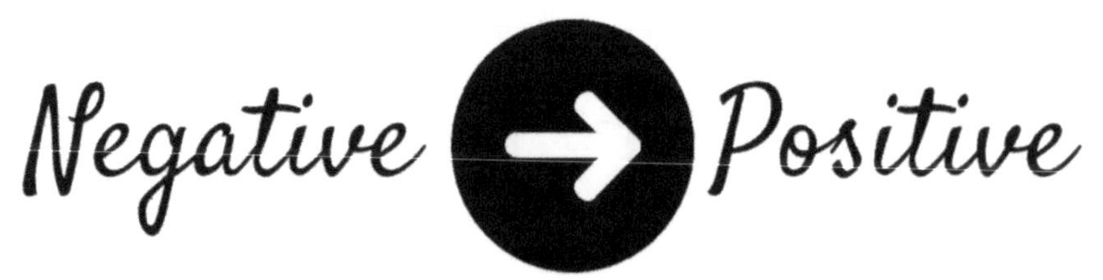

My negative thought: _______________________

____

____

____

Evidence for my thought:

Evidence against my thought:

How can I reframe my negative thought to a more realistic one?

____

____

____

____

Anxiety Journal

DATE & TIME _______________________________

PLACE _______________________ SOURCE OF ANXIETY _______________________

NEGATIVE BELIEFS

ABOUT SITUATION:

ABOUT YOURSELF:

WHAT FACTS ARE TRUE

ABOUT SITUATION:

ABOUT YOURSELF:

WHAT HAPPENED AND HOW I FEEL

HOW DID I REACT & WHAT HELPS ME TO CALM

Negative → Positive

My negative thought: _______________________

____

____

____

____

Evidence for my thought:

Evidence against my thought:

Anxiety Journal

DATE & TIME ________________________________

PLACE ____________________ SOURCE OF ANXIETY ____________________

NEGATIVE BELIEFS

ABOUT SITUATION:

ABOUT YOURSELF:

WHAT FACTS ARE TRUE

ABOUT SITUATION:

ABOUT YOURSELF:

WHAT HAPPENED AND HOW I FEEL

HOW DID I REACT & WHAT HELPS ME TO CALM

My negative thought: _______________________

____

____

____

____

Evidence for my thought:

Evidence against my thought:

How can I reframe my negative thought to a more realistic one?

Anxiety Journal

DATE & TIME _______________________________________

PLACE ___________________________ SOURCE OF ANXIETY _______________________

NEGATIVE BELIEFS

ABOUT SITUATION:

ABOUT YOURSELF:

WHAT FACTS ARE TRUE

ABOUT SITUATION:

ABOUT YOURSELF:

WHAT HAPPENED AND HOW I FEEL

HOW DID I REACT & WHAT HELPS ME TO CALM

Negative  Positive

My negative thought: ______________________________

____

____

____

____

Evidence for my thought:

Evidence against my thought:

How can I reframe my negative thought to a more realistic one?

Anxiety Journal

DATE & TIME ____

PLACE ______________________ SOURCE OF ANXIETY _________________________

NEGATIVE BELIEFS

ABOUT SITUATION:

ABOUT YOURSELF:

WHAT FACTS ARE TRUE

ABOUT SITUATION:

ABOUT YOURSELF:

WHAT HAPPENED AND HOW I FEEL

HOW DID I REACT & WHAT HELPS ME TO CALM

Negative → Positive

My negative thought: _______________________

____

____

____

____

Evidence for my thought:

Evidence against my thought:

How can I reframe my negative thought to a more realistic one?

____

____

____

____

____

Anxiety Journal

DATE & TIME ________________________________

PLACE ____________________________ SOURCE OF ANXIETY ____________________

NEGATIVE BELIEFS

ABOUT SITUATION:

ABOUT YOURSELF:

WHAT FACTS ARE TRUE

ABOUT SITUATION:

ABOUT YOURSELF:

WHAT HAPPENED AND HOW I FEEL

HOW DID I REACT & WHAT HELPS ME TO CALM

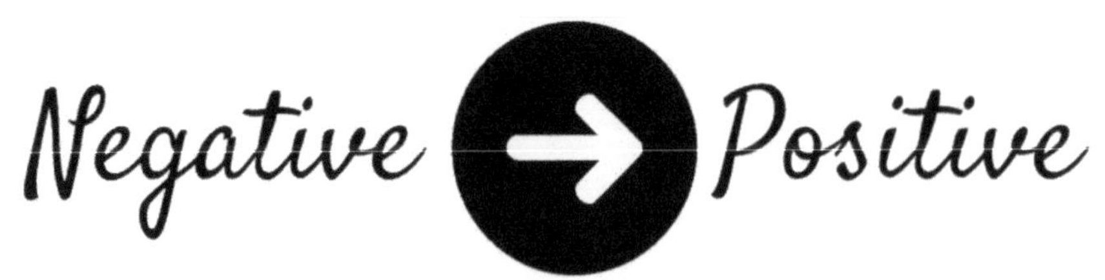 Negative → Positive

My negative thought: _______________________

____

____

____

____

Evidence for my thought: Evidence against my thought:

How can I reframe my negative thought to a more realistic one?

Anxiety Journal

DATE & TIME _______________________________

PLACE ___________________________ SOURCE OF ANXIETY _______________

NEGATIVE BELIEFS

ABOUT SITUATION:

ABOUT YOURSELF:

WHAT FACTS ARE TRUE

ABOUT SITUATION:

ABOUT YOURSELF:

WHAT HAPPENED AND HOW I FEEL

HOW DID I REACT & WHAT HELPS ME TO CALM

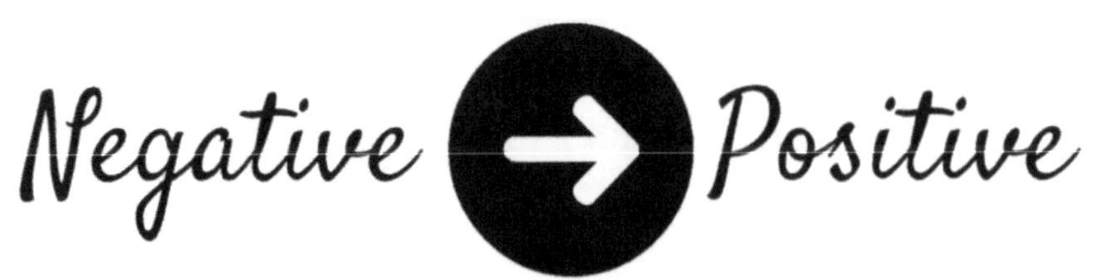

My negative thought: _______________________

____

____

____

____

Evidence for my thought:

Evidence against my thought:

How can I reframe my negative thought to a more realistic one?

____

____

____

____

____

www.ingramcontent.com/pod-product-compliance
Lightning Source LLC
Chambersburg PA
CBHW041832110726
48006CB00020B/2601